God Comforts You

PROMISE JOURNAL

God Comforts You
© 2007 Ellie Claire, Inc.

Compiled by Joanie Garborg
Designed by Mick Thurber

Scripture references are from the following sources: The Holy Bible, King James Version (KJV). The Holy Bible, New International Version (NIV). Copyright © 1973, 1978, 1984 International Bible Society. Used by permission of Zondervan Bible Publishers. The New American Standard Bible® (NASB), Copyright © 1960, 1962, 1963, 1968, 1971, 1972, 1973, 1975, 1977, 1995 by The Lockman Foundation. Used by permission. The Holy Bible, New Living Translation (NLT), copyright 1996. Used by permission of Tyndale House Publishers, Inc., Wheaton, Illinois 60189. All rights reserved. The Message (MSG). Copyright © 1994, 1994, 1995, 1996, 2000, 2001, 2002. Used by permission of NavPress Publishing Group. The New Revised Standard Version Bible: Anglicized Edition (NRSV), copyright 1989, 1995, Division of Christian Education of the National Council of the Churches of Christ in the United States of America. Used by permission. All rights reserved. The Living Bible (TLB) © 1971. Used by permission of Tyndale House Publishers, Inc., Wheaton, Illinois 60189. All rights reserved.

Excluding Scripture verses, references to men and masculine pronouns have been replaced with gender-neutral references.

ISBN-10: 0-9794446-0-8
ISBN-13: 978-0-9794446-0-9

To:

_____

From:

_____

_____

THE WEAVER

My life is but a weaving
Between my Lord and me,
I cannot choose the colors
He worketh steadily.
Oftimes He weaveth sorrow,
And I in foolish pride

Forget He sees the upper
And I, the underside....
The dark threads are as needful
In the Weaver's skillful hand
As the threads of gold and silver
In the pattern He has planned.

There may be times in your life when it all seems dark and you cannot see or trace the hand of God, but yet God is working. Just as much as He works in the bright sunlight, He works all through the night.

There are those who suffer greatly, and yet, through the recognition that pain can be a thread in the pattern of God's weaving, find the way to a fundamental joy.

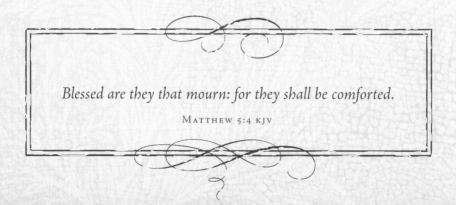

Blessed are they that mourn: for they shall be comforted.

MATTHEW 5:4 KJV

THE WEAVER

_____

_____

_____

_____

_____

_____

_____

_____

_____

_____

_____

_____

_____

_____

_____

_____

_____

_____

_____

_____

_____

Blessed be the God and Father of our Lord Jesus Christ, the Father of mercies and God of all comfort, who comforts us in all our affliction so that we will be able to comfort those who are in any affliction with the comfort with which we ourselves are comforted by God.

2 CORINTHIANS 1:3–4 KJV

May our Lord Jesus Christ and God our Father, who loved us and in his special favor gave us everlasting comfort and good hope, comfort your hearts and give you strength in every good thing you do and say.

2 THESSALONIANS 2:16–17 NLT

I, even I, am he who comforts you.

ISAIAH 51:12 NIV

> *Only God can truly comfort; He comes alongside*
> *us and shows us how deeply and tenderly He feels*
> *for us in our sorrow.*

COMFORTED BY GOD

_____

_____

_____

_____

_____

_____

_____

_____

_____

_____

_____

_____

_____

_____

_____

_____

_____

_____

_____

_____

_____

TREASURE IN NATURE

If we are children of God, we have a tremendous treasure in nature and will realize that it is holy and sacred. We will see God reaching out to us in every wind that blows, every sunrise and sunset, every cloud in the sky, every flower that blooms, and every leaf that fades.

OSWALD CHAMBERS

The longer I live, the more my mind dwells upon the beauty and the wonder of the world.

JOHN BURROUGHS

Look up at all the stars in the night sky and hear your Father saying, "I carefully set each one in its place. Know that I love you more than these." Sit by the lake's edge, listening to the water lapping the shore and hear your Father gently calling you to that place near His heart.

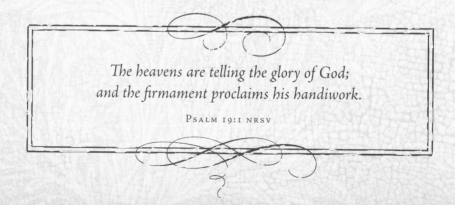

The heavens are telling the glory of God;
and the firmament proclaims his handiwork.

PSALM 19:1 NRSV

TREASURE IN NATURE

THE GRACE OF GOD

But God, being rich in mercy, because of His great love with which He loved us, even when we were dead in our transgressions, made us alive together with Christ (by grace you have been saved), and raised us up with Him, and seated us with Him in the heavenly places in Christ Jesus, so that in the ages to come He might show the surpassing riches of His grace in kindness toward us in Christ Jesus. For by grace you have been saved through faith; and that not of yourselves, it is the gift of God; not as a result of works, so that no one may boast. For we are His workmanship, created in Christ Jesus for good works, which God prepared beforehand so that we would walk in them.

EPHESIANS 2:4–10 NASB

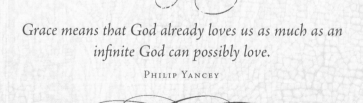

Grace means that God already loves us as much as an infinite God can possibly love.

PHILIP YANCEY

THE GRACE OF GOD

In the Silence

Our Father, sometimes Thou dost seem so far away, as if Thou art a God in hiding, as if Thou art determined to elude all who seek Thee…. At times when we feel forsaken, may we know the presence of the Holy Spirit who brings comfort to all human hearts when we are willing to surrender ourselves.

Peter Marshall

I believe in the sun even when it is not shining.

I believe in love even when I do not feel it.

I believe in God even when He is silent.

On a wall where Jews were hidden in WWII

Be it ours, when we cannot see the face of God, to trust under the shadow of His wings.

Charles H. Spurgeon

The eternal God is your refuge,
and underneath are the everlasting arms.

Deuteronomy 33:27 niv

IN THE SILENCE

_____

_____

_____

_____

_____

_____

_____

_____

_____

_____

_____

_____

_____

_____

_____

_____

_____

_____

_____

_____

_____

GOD'S GUIDANCE

To You, O Lord, I lift up my soul. O my God, in You I trust, do not let me be ashamed; do not let my enemies exult over me. Indeed, none of those who wait for You will be ashamed…. Make me know Your ways, O Lord; teach me Your paths. Lead me in Your truth and teach me, for You are the God of my salvation; for You I wait all the day. Remember, O Lord, Your compassion and Your lovingkindnesses, for they have been from of old.

PSALM 25:1–6 NASB

You will keep on guiding me with your counsel, leading me to a glorious destiny.

PSALM 73:24 NLT

The Lord is able to guide. The promises cover every imaginable situation…. Take the hand He stretches out.

ELISABETH ELLIOT

GOD'S GUIDANCE

_____
_____
_____
_____
_____
_____
_____
_____
_____
_____
_____
_____
_____
_____
_____
_____
_____
_____
_____

THE GOODNESS OF GOD

The goodness of God is infinitely more wonderful than we will ever be able to comprehend.

A. W. TOZER

All that is good, all that is true, all that is beautiful, all that is beneficent, be it great or small, be it perfect or fragmentary, natural as well as supernatural, moral as well as material, comes from God.

CARDINAL JOHN HENRY NEWMAN

We walk without fear, full of hope and courage and strength to do His will, waiting for the endless good which He is always giving as fast as He can get us able to take it in.

GEORGE MacDONALD

Open your mouth and taste, open your eyes and see—how good God is. Blessed are you who run to him. Worship God if you want the best; worship opens doors to all his goodness.

PSALM 34:8–9 MSG

THE GOODNESS OF GOD

_____

_____

_____

_____

_____

_____

_____

_____

_____

_____

_____

_____

_____

_____

_____

_____

_____

_____

THE MAJESTY OF GOD

O Lord, our Lord, how majestic is your name in all the earth! You have set your glory above the heavens.... When I consider your heavens, the work of your fingers, the moon and the stars, which you have set in place, what is man that you are mindful of him, the son of man that you care for him? You made him a little lower than the heavenly beings and crowned him with glory and honor. O Lord, our Lord, how majestic is your name in all the earth!

PSALM 8:1–5, 9 NIV

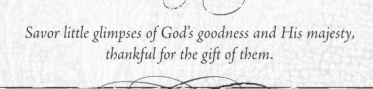

Savor little glimpses of God's goodness and His majesty,
thankful for the gift of them.

THE MAJESTY OF GOD

_____

_____

_____

_____

_____

_____

_____

_____

_____

_____

_____

_____

_____

_____

_____

_____

_____

_____

_____

_____

_____

_____

Place of Rest

Breathe, O breathe thy loving Spirit into every troubled breast;

Let us all in thee inherit, let us find thy promised rest.

Charles Wesley

Trust Him when dark doubts assail thee

Trust Him when thy strength is small,

Trust Him when to simply trust Him

Seems the hardest thing of all.

Trust Him, He is ever faithful;

Trust Him, for His will is best;

Trust Him, for the Heart of Jesus,

Is the only place of rest.

In returning and rest shall ye be saved;
in quietness and in confidence shall be your strength.

Isaiah 30:15 KJV

Place of Rest

GOD UNDERSTANDS

He heals the brokenhearted, binding up their wounds. He counts the stars and calls them all by name. How great is our Lord! His power is absolute! His understanding is beyond comprehension! The Lord's delight is in those who honor him, those who put their hope in his unfailing love.

PSALM 147:3–5, 11 NLT

Trust in the Lord with all thine heart; and lean not unto thine own understanding. In all thy ways acknowledge him, and he shall direct thy paths.

PROVERBS 3:5–6 KJV

Our help is in the name of the Lord, who made heaven and earth.

PSALM 124:8 KJV

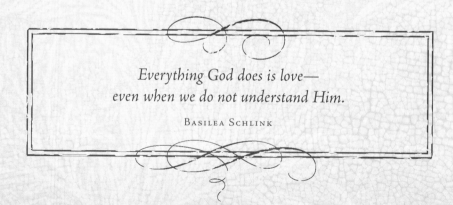

Everything God does is love—
even when we do not understand Him.

BASILEA SCHLINK

GOD UNDERSTANDS

MADE FOR JOY

Our hearts were made for joy. Our hearts were made to enjoy the One who created them. Too deeply planted to be much affected by the ups and downs of life, this joy is a knowing and a being known by our Creator. He sets our hearts alight with radiant joy.

If one is joyful, it means that one is faithfully living for God, and that nothing else counts; and if one gives joy to others one is doing God's work. With joy without and joy within, all is well.

JANET ERSKINE STUART

Live for today but hold your hands open to tomorrow. Anticipate the future and its changes with joy. There is a seed of God's love in every event, every circumstance, every unpleasant situation in which you may find yourself.

BARBARA JOHNSON

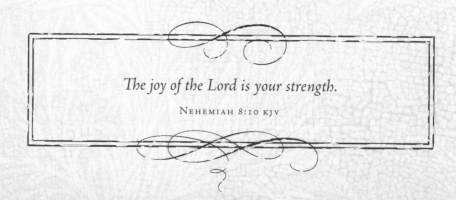

The joy of the Lord is your strength.

NEHEMIAH 8:10 KJV

MADE FOR JOY

LOVE LIKE THAT

Watch what God does, and then you do it, like children who learn proper behavior from their parents. Mostly what God does is love you. Keep company with him and learn a life of love. Observe how Christ loved us. His love was not cautious but extravagant. He didn't love in order to get something from us but to give everything of himself to us. Love like that.

EPHESIANS 5:1–2 MSG

I pray that your love for each other will overflow more and more, and that you will keep on growing in your knowledge and understanding.

PHILIPPIANS 1:9 NLT

*Open your hearts to the love God instills.... God loves you
tenderly. What He gives you is not to be kept under lock
and key, but to be shared.*

MOTHER TERESA

LOVE LIKE THAT

_____

_____

_____

_____

_____

_____

_____

_____

_____

_____

_____

_____

_____

_____

_____

_____

_____

_____

MIGHTY TO KEEP

God is adequate as our keeper.... Your faith will not fail while God sustains it; you are not strong enough to fall away while God is resolved to hold you.

J. I. PACKER

I place no hope in my strength…but all my confidence is in God my protector, who never abandons those who have put all their hope and thought in Him.

FRANÇOIS RABELAIS

God, who is our dwelling place, is also our fortress. It can only mean one thing, and that is, that if we will but live in our dwelling place, we shall be perfectly safe and secure from every assault.

HANNAH WHITALL SMITH

He who dwells in the shelter of the Most High will abide in the shadow of the Almighty. I will say to the Lord, "My refuge and my fortress, My God, in whom I trust!"

PSALM 91:1–2 NASB

MIGHTY TO KEEP

_____

_____

_____

_____

_____

_____

_____

_____

_____

_____

_____

_____

_____

_____

_____

_____

_____

_____

_____

_____

A SAFE JOURNEY

He rescues you from hidden traps, shields you from deadly hazards. His huge outstretched arms protect you—under them you're perfectly safe; his arms fend off all harm. Fear nothing—not wild wolves in the night, not flying arrows in the day, not disease that prowls through the darkness, not disaster that erupts at high noon…."If you'll hold on to me for dear life," says God, "I'll get you out of any trouble. I'll give you the best of care if you'll only get to know and trust me. Call me and I'll answer, be at your side in bad times."

PSALM 91:3–6, 14 MSG

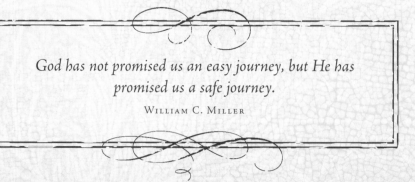

God has not promised us an easy journey, but He has promised us a safe journey.

WILLIAM C. MILLER

A SAFE JOURNEY

_____

_____

_____

_____

_____

_____

_____

_____

_____

_____

_____

_____

_____

_____

_____

_____

_____

_____

_____

_____

A LIFE TRANSFORMED

To pray is to change. This is a great grace. How good of God to provide a path whereby our lives can be taken over by love and joy and peace and patience and kindness and goodness and faithfulness and gentleness and self-control.

RICHARD J. FOSTER

For God is, indeed, a wonderful Father who longs to pour out His mercy upon us, and whose majesty is so great that He can transform us from deep within.

TERESA OF AVILA

A life transformed by the power of God is always a marvel and a miracle.

GERALDINE NICHOLAS

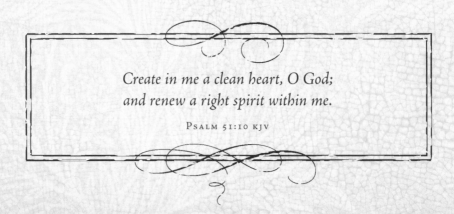

Create in me a clean heart, O God;
and renew a right spirit within me.

PSALM 51:10 KJV

A LIFE TRANSFORMED

GOD'S COMPASSION

It is of the Lord's mercies that we are not consumed, because his compassions fail not. They are new every morning: great is thy faithfulness. The Lord is my portion, saith my soul; therefore will I hope in him. The Lord is good unto them that wait for him, to the soul that seeketh him. For the Lord will not cast off for ever: But though he cause grief, yet will he have compassion according to the multitude of his mercies. For he doth not afflict willingly nor grieve the children of men.

LAMENTATIONS 3:22–24, 31–33 KJV

Lord, don't hold back your tender mercies from me. My only hope is in your unfailing love and faithfulness.

PSALM 40:11 NLT

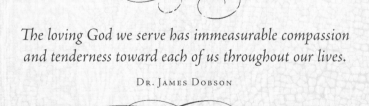

The loving God we serve has immeasurable compassion
and tenderness toward each of us throughout our lives.

DR. JAMES DOBSON

GOD'S COMPASSION

OVERCOMING

Christ desires to be with you in whatever crisis you may find yourself. Call upon His name. See if He will not do as He promised He would. He will not make your problems go away, but He will give you the power to deal with and overcome them.... Suffering is endurable if we do not have to bear it alone; and the more compassionate the Presence, the less acute the pain.

BILLY GRAHAM

He did not say, "You will never have a rough passage, you will never be over-strained, you will never feel uncomfortable," but He did say, "You will never be overcome."

JULIAN OF NORWICH

The world is full of suffering. It is also full of the overcoming of it.

HELEN KELLER

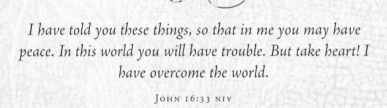

I have told you these things, so that in me you may have peace. In this world you will have trouble. But take heart! I have overcome the world.

JOHN 16:33 NIV

OVERCOMING

_____

_____

_____

_____

_____

_____

_____

_____

_____

_____

_____

_____

_____

_____

_____

_____

_____

_____

_____

_____

_____

_____

_____

_____

_____

GOD'S PEACE

Let not your heart be troubled: ye believe in God, believe also in me. In my Father's house are many mansions: if it were not so, I would have told you. I go to prepare a place for you. And if I go and prepare a place for you, I will come again, and receive you unto myself; that where I am, there ye may be also. I will not leave you comfortless: I will come to you. Peace I leave with you, my peace I give unto you: not as the world giveth, give I unto you. Let not your heart be troubled, neither let it be afraid.

JOHN 14:1–3, 18, 27 KJV

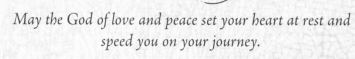

May the God of love and peace set your heart at rest and speed you on your journey.

RAYMOND OF PENYAFORT

GOD'S PEACE

By Love Alone

By love alone is God enjoyed; by love alone delighted in, by love alone approached and admired. His nature requires love.

Thomas Traherne

Love does not allow lovers
to belong anymore to themselves,
but they belong only to the Beloved.

Dionysius

There is an essential connection between experiencing God, loving God, and trusting God. You will trust God only as much as you love Him, and you will love Him to the extent you have touched Him, rather than He has touched you.

Brennan Manning

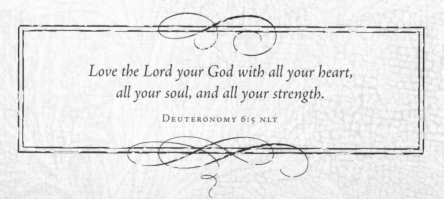

Love the Lord your God with all your heart,
all your soul, and all your strength.

Deuteronomy 6:5 nlt

BY LOVE ALONE

RESTORATION

The Spirit of the Sovereign Lord is on me, because the Lord has anointed me to preach good news to the poor. He has sent me to bind up the brokenhearted, to proclaim freedom for the captives and release from darkness for the prisoners, to proclaim the year of the Lord's favor and the day of vengeance of our God, to comfort all who mourn, and provide for those who grieve in Zion—to bestow on them a crown of beauty instead of ashes, the oil of gladness instead of mourning, and a garment of praise instead of a spirit of despair. They will be called oaks of righteousness, a planting of the Lord for the display of his splendor.

ISAIAH 61:1–3 NIV

The Lord promises to bind up the brokenhearted, to give relief and full deliverance to those whose spirits have been weighed down.

CHARLES R. SWINDOLL

RESTORATION

_____

_____

_____

_____

_____

_____

_____

_____

_____

_____

_____

_____

_____

_____

_____

_____

_____

_____

STEPS OF FAITH

In the dark dreary nights, when the storm is at its most fierce, the lighthouse burns bright so the sailors can find their way home again. In life the same light burns. This light is fueled with love, faith, and hope. And through life's most fierce storms these three burn their brightest so we also can find our way home again.

Why should we live halfway up the hill and swathed in the mists, when we might have an unclouded sky and a radiant sun over our heads if we would climb higher and walk in the light of His face?

ALEXANDER MACLAREN

Faith goes up the stairs that love has made and looks out the window which hope has opened.

CHARLES H. SPURGEON

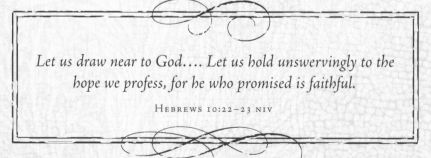

Let us draw near to God.... Let us hold unswervingly to the hope we profess, for he who promised is faithful.

HEBREWS 10:22–23 NIV

STEPS OF FAITH

Remember your promise to me, for it is my only hope. Your promise revives me; it comforts me in all my troubles…. I meditate on your age-old laws; O Lord, they comfort me…. Your principles have been the music of my life throughout the years of my pilgrimage. I reflect at night on who you are, O Lord, and I obey your law because of this…. Forever, O Lord, your word stands firm in heaven. Your faithfulness extends to every generation, as enduring as the earth you created. Your laws remain true today.

PSALM 119:49–55, 89–91 NLT

Swim through your troubles. Run to the promises, they are our Lord's branches hanging over the water so that His children may take a grip of them.

SAMUEL RUTHERFORD

FAITHFULNESS EXTENDED

ENFOLDED IN PEACE

I will let God's peace infuse every part of today. As the chaos swirls and life's demands pull at me on all sides, I will breathe in God's peace that surpasses all understanding. He has promised that He would set within me a peace too deeply planted to be affected by unexpected or exhausting demands.

Calm me, O Lord, as you stilled the storm,

Still me, O Lord, keep me from harm.

Let all the tumult within me cease,

Enfold me, Lord, in your peace.

CELTIC TRADITIONAL

God cannot give us a happiness and peace apart from himself, because it is not there. There is no such thing.

C. S. LEWIS

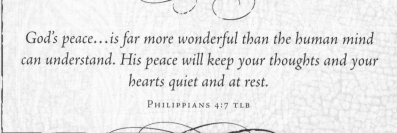

God's peace...is far more wonderful than the human mind can understand. His peace will keep your thoughts and your hearts quiet and at rest.

PHILIPPIANS 4:7 TLB

E N F O L D E D   I N   P E A C E

Seek First

Look at the birds of the air, that they do not sow, nor reap nor gather into barns, and yet your heavenly Father feeds them. Are you not worth much more than they? And who of you by being worried can add a single hour to his life? And why are you worried about clothing? Observe how the lilies of the field grow; they do not toil nor do they spin, yet I say to you that not even Solomon in all his glory clothed himself like one of these. But if God so clothes the grass of the field, which is alive today and tomorrow is thrown into the furnace, will He not much more clothe you? You of little faith! Do not worry then, saying, "What will we eat?" or "What will we drink?" or "What will we wear for clothing?" For…your heavenly Father knows that you need all these things. But seek first His kingdom and His righteousness, and all these things will be added to you.

Matthew 6:26–33 nasb

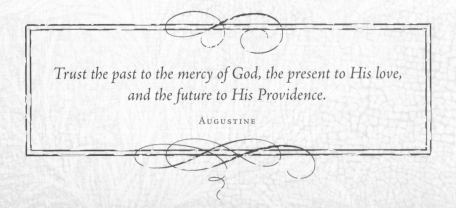

Trust the past to the mercy of God, the present to His love,
and the future to His Providence.

Augustine

SEEK FIRST

_____

_____

_____

_____

_____

_____

_____

_____

_____

_____

_____

_____

_____

_____

_____

_____

_____

_____

_____

_____

_____

_____

SHINING PROMISES

Our feelings do not affect God's facts. They may blow up, like clouds, and cover the eternal things that we do most truly believe. We may not see the shining of the promises—but they still shine! [His strength] is not for one moment less because of our human weakness.

AMY CARMICHAEL

> God's ways seem dark, but soon or late,
> They touch the shining hills of day.

JOHN GREENLEAF WHITTIER

We do not know how this is true—where would faith be if we did?—but we do know that all things that happen are full of shining seed. Light is sown for us—not darkness.

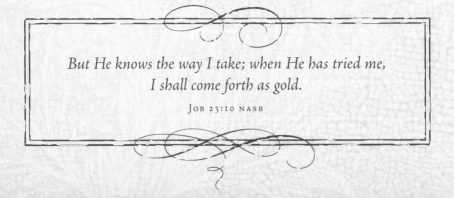

But He knows the way I take; when He has tried me,
I shall come forth as gold.

JOB 23:10 NASB

SHINING PROMISES

By Faith

Now faith is being sure of what we hope for and certain of what we do not see. By faith we understand that the universe was formed at God's command, so that what is seen was not made out of what was visible. And without faith it is impossible to please God, because anyone who comes to him must believe that he exists and that he rewards those who earnestly seek him.

Hebrews 11:1, 3, 6 niv

Faith, as the Bible defines it, is present-tense action. Faith means being sure of what we hope for…now. It means knowing something is real, this moment, all around you, even when you don't see it. Great faith isn't the ability to believe long and far into the misty future. It's simply taking God at His word and taking the next step.

Joni Eareckson Tada

BY FAITH

TRUST GOD'S HEART

He writes in characters too grand
for our short sight to understand.
We catch but broken strokes
and try to fathom all the withered hopes
Of death, of life,
the endless war, the useless strife....
But there, with larger, clearer sight, we shall see this:
His way was right.

JOHN OXENHAM

In those times I can't seem to find God, I rest in the assurance He knows how to find me.

NEVA COYLE

Wait upon God's strengthening, and say to Him, "O Lord, You have been our refuge in all generations." Trust in Him who has placed this burden on you. What you yourself cannot bear, bear with the help of God who is all-powerful.

BONIFACE

Lord, You have been our dwelling place in all generations....
Even from everlasting to everlasting, You are God.

PSALM 90:1–2 NASB

TRUST GOD'S HEART

_____

_____

_____

_____

_____

_____

_____

_____

_____

_____

_____

_____

_____

_____

_____

_____

_____

_____

_____

_____

_____

_____

_____

_____

THE STRONGHOLD

The Lord is my light and my salvation—whom shall I fear? The Lord is the stronghold of my life—of whom shall I be afraid? One thing I ask of the Lord, this is what I seek: that I may dwell in the house of the Lord all the days of my life, to gaze upon the beauty of the Lord and to seek him in his temple. For in the day of trouble he will keep me safe in his dwelling; he will hide me in the shelter of his tabernacle and set me high upon a rock. Hear my voice when I call, O Lord; be merciful to me and answer me. My heart says of you, "Seek his face!" Your face, Lord, I will seek.

PSALM 27:1, 4–5, 7–8 NIV

Leave behind your fear and dwell on the lovingkindness of God, that you may recover by gazing on Him.

THE STRONGHOLD

GRACE FOR TRIALS

God has not promised skies always blue,

flower-strewn pathways all our lives through;

God has not promised sun without rain,

joy without sorrow, peace without pain.

But God has promised strength for the day,

rest for the labor, light for the way,

grace for the trials, help from above,

unfailing sympathy, undying love.

ANNIE JOHNSON FLINT

After winter comes the summer. After night comes the dawn. And after every storm,

there comes clear, open skies.

SAMUEL RUTHERFORD

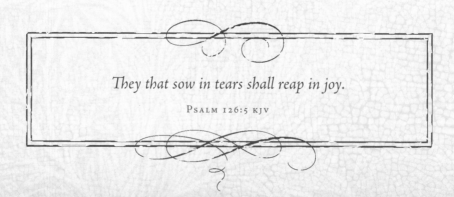

They that sow in tears shall reap in joy.

PSALM 126:5 KJV

GRACE FOR TRIALS

_____

_____

_____

_____

_____

_____

_____

_____

_____

_____

_____

_____

_____

_____

_____

_____

_____

_____

_____

_____

_____

RENEWED STRENGTH

Why do you say.... "My way is hidden from the Lord; my cause is disregarded by my God"? Do you not know? Have you not heard? The Lord is the everlasting God, the Creator of the ends of the earth. He will not grow tired or weary, and his understanding no one can fathom. Even youths grow tired and weary, and young men stumble and fall; but those who hope in the Lord will renew their strength. They will soar on wings like eagles; they will run and not grow weary, they will walk and not be faint.

ISAIAH 40:27–31 NIV

Come, let us go up to the mountain of the Lord, to the house of the God of Jacob. He will teach us his ways, so that we may walk in his paths

ISAIAH 2:3 NIV

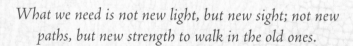

What we need is not new light, but new sight; not new paths, but new strength to walk in the old ones.

RENEWED STRENGTH

COUNTLESS BEAUTIES

May God give you eyes to see beauty only the heart can understand.

From the world we see, hear, and touch, we behold inspired visions that reveal God's glory. In the sun's light, we catch warm rays of grace and glimpse His eternal design. In the birds' song, we hear His voice and it reawakens our desire for Him. At the wind's touch, we feel His Spirit and sense our eternal existence.

All the world is an utterance of the Almighty. Its countless beauties, its exquisite adaptations, all speak to you of Him.

PHILLIPS BROOKS

Worship the Lord in the beauty of holiness.

PSALM 96:9 NIV

COUNTLESS BEAUTIES

DON'T BE AFRAID

Don't be afraid, I've redeemed you. I've called your name. You're mine. When you're in over your head, I'll be there with you. When you're in rough waters, you will not go down. When you're between a rock and a hard place, it won't be a dead end— Because I am God, your personal God, The Holy of Israel, your Savior. I paid a huge price for you…! *That's* how much you mean to me! *That's* how much I love you!

ISAIAH 43:1–4 MSG

Do not be afraid to enter the cloud that is settling down on your life. God is in it. The other side is radiant with His glory.

L. B. COWMAN

DON'T BE AFRAID

SEEING BY FAITH

Living a life of faith means never knowing where you are being led. But it does mean loving and knowing the One who is leading. It is literally a life of faith, not of understanding and reason—a life of knowing Him who calls us to go.

OSWALD CHAMBERS

Where reasons are given, we don't need faith. Where only darkness surrounds us, we have no means for seeing except by faith.

ELISABETH ELLIOT

Trust God where you cannot trace Him. Do not try to penetrate the cloud He brings over you; rather look to the bow that is on it. The mystery is God's; the promise is yours.

JOHN MacDUFF

The secret things belong unto the Lord our God:
but those things which are revealed belong unto
us and to our children for ever.

DEUTERONOMY 29:29 KJV

SEEING BY FAITH

GOD'S POWER

I pray that out of his glorious riches he may strengthen you with power through his Spirit in your inner being, so that Christ may dwell in your hearts through faith. And I pray that you, being rooted and established in love, may have power, together with all the saints, to grasp how wide and long and high and deep is the love of Christ, and to know this love that surpasses knowledge—that you may be filled to the measure of all the fullness of God. Now to him who is able to do immeasurably more than all we ask or imagine, according to his power that is at work within us, to him be glory in the church and in Christ Jesus throughout all generations, for ever and ever! Amen.

EPHESIANS 3:16–21 NIV

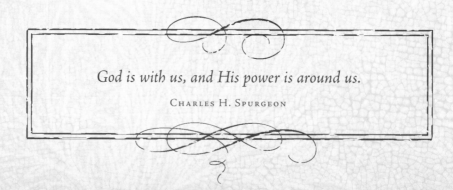

God is with us, and His power is around us.

CHARLES H. SPURGEON

GOD'S POWER

_____

_____

_____

_____

_____

_____

_____

_____

_____

_____

_____

_____

_____

_____

_____

_____

_____

_____

_____

_____

_____

_____

Nothing but Grace

There is nothing but God's grace. We walk upon it; we breathe it; we live and die by it; it makes the nails and axles of the universe.

Robert Louis Stevenson

Grace is no stationary thing, it is ever becoming. It is flowing straight out of God's heart. Grace does nothing but re-form and convey God. Grace makes the soul conformable to the will of God. God, the ground of the soul, and grace go together.

Meister Eckhart

Grace and gratitude belong together like heaven and earth. Grace evokes gratitude like the voice an echo. Gratitude follows grace as thunder follows lightning.

Karl Barth

God is sheer mercy and grace; not easily angered,
he's rich in love.... As far as sunrise is from sunset,
he has separated us from our sins.

Psalm 103:8, 12 MSG

NOTHING BUT GRACE

SHOWERS OF BLESSINGS

Bless the Lord, O my soul: and all that is within me, bless his holy name. Bless the Lord, O my soul, and forget not all his benefits: Who forgiveth all thine iniquities; who healeth all thy diseases; who redeemeth thy life from destruction; who crowneth thee with lovingkindness and tender mercies; who satisfieth thy mouth with good things; so that thy youth is renewed like the eagle's.

PSALM 103:1–5 KJV

I will send showers, showers of blessings, which will come just when they are needed.

EZEKIEL 34:26 NLT

God, who is love—who is, if I may say it this way, made out of love—simply cannot help but shed blessing on blessing upon us.

HANNAH WHITALL SMITH

SHOWERS OF BLESSINGS

GOD KNOWS

The simple fact of being…in the presence of the Lord and of showing Him all that I think, feel, sense, and experience, without trying to hide anything, must please Him. Somehow, somewhere, I know that He loves me, even though I do not feel that love as I can feel a human embrace, even though I do not hear a voice as I hear human words of consolation…. God is greater than my senses, greater than my thoughts, greater than my heart. I do believe that He touches me in places that are unknown even to myself.

HENRI J. M. NOUWEN

Pour out your heart to God your Father. He understands you better than you do.

God possesses infinite knowledge and an awareness which is uniquely His. At all times, even in the midst of any type of suffering, I can realize that He knows, loves, watches, understands, and more than that, He has a purpose.

BILLY GRAHAM

The person who loves God is the one God knows and cares for.

1 CORINTHIANS 8:3 NLT

GOD KNOWS

_____

_____

_____

_____

_____

_____

_____

_____

_____

_____

_____

_____

_____

_____

_____

_____

_____

_____

_____

_____

GOD'S ETERNAL LOVE

The Lord is like a father to his children, tender and compassionate to those who fear him. For he understands how weak we are; he knows we are only dust. Our days on earth are like grass; like wildflowers, we bloom and die. The wind blows, and we are gone—as though we had never been here. But the love of the Lord remains forever…. The Lord has made the heavens his throne; from there he rules over everything.

PSALM 103:13–17, 19 NLT

He remembered our utter weakness. His faithful love endures forever.

PSALM 136:23 NLT

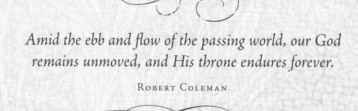

Amid the ebb and flow of the passing world, our God remains unmoved, and His throne endures forever.

ROBERT COLEMAN

GOD'S ETERNAL LOVE

LIFT UP YOUR EYES

It should fill us with joy, that infinite wisdom guides the affairs of the world…that infinite wisdom directs every event, brings order out of confusion, and light out of darkness, and, to those who love God, causes all things, whatever be their present aspect and apparent tendency, to work together for good.

J. L. DAGG

I lift up mine eyes to the quiet hills,
and my heart to the Father's throne;
in all my ways, to the end of days,
the Lord will preserve His own.

TIMOTHY DUDLEY-SMITH

Faith is to believe what we do not see; and the reward of this faith is to see what we believe.

AUGUSTINE

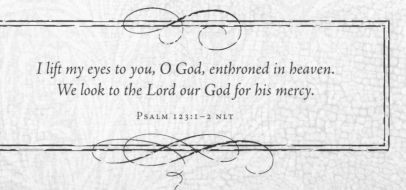

I lift my eyes to you, O God, enthroned in heaven.
We look to the Lord our God for his mercy.

PSALM 123:1–2 NLT

LIFT UP YOUR EYES

LOVE NEVER FAILS

If I speak with the tongues of men and of angels, but do not have love, I have become a noisy gong or a clanging cymbal. If I have the gift of prophecy, and know all mysteries and all knowledge; and if I have all faith, so as to remove mountains, but do not have love, I am nothing. And if I give all my possessions to feed the poor, and if I surrender my body to be burned, but do not have love, it profits me nothing. Love is patient, love is kind and is not jealous; love does not brag and is not arrogant, does not act unbecomingly; it does not seek its own, is not provoked, does not take into account a wrong suffered, does not rejoice in unrighteousness, but rejoices with the truth; bears all things, believes all things, hopes all things, endures all things. Love never fails.

1 CORINTHIANS 13:1–8 NASB

An instant of pure love is more precious to God…than all other good works together.

JOHN OF THE CROSS

L O V E N E V E R F A I L S

FOR HIMSELF

Although it be good to think upon the kindness of God, and to love Him and worship Him for it; yet it is far better to gaze upon the pure essence of Him and to love Him and worship Him for himself.

We desire many things, and God offers us only one thing. He can offer us only one thing—himself. He has nothing else to give. There is nothing else to give.

PETER KREEFT

The reason for loving God is God himself, and the measure in which we should love Him is to love Him without measure.

BERNARD OF CLAIRVAUX

The Lord alone shall be exalted.

ISAIAH 2:11 KJV

F O R   H I M S E L F

GOD'S CARE

The Lord is my shepherd; I shall not want. He maketh me to lie down in green pastures: he leadeth me beside the still waters. He restoreth my soul: he leadeth me in the paths of righteousness for his name's sake. Yea, though I walk through the valley of the shadow of death, I will fear no evil: for thou art with me; thy rod and thy staff they comfort me. Thou preparest a table before me in the presence of mine enemies: thou anointest my head with oil; my cup runneth over. Surely goodness and mercy shall follow me all the days of my life: and I will dwell in the house of the Lord for ever.

PSALM 23:1–6 KJV

God never abandons anyone on whom He has set His love; nor does Christ, the good shepherd, ever lose track of His sheep.

J. I. PACKER

GOD'S CARE

_____

_____

_____

_____

_____

_____

_____

_____

_____

_____

_____

_____

_____

_____

_____

_____

_____

_____

_____

_____

_____

_____

_____

His Imprint

The God of the universe—the One who created everything and holds it all in His hand—created each of us in His image, to bear His likeness, His imprint. It is only when Christ dwells within our hearts, radiating the pure light of His love through our humanity that we discover who we are and what we were intended to be.

In the very beginning it was God who formed us by His Word. He made us in His own image. God was spirit and He gave us a spirit so that He could come into us and mingle His own life with our life.

MADAME JEANNE GUYON

Made in His image, we can have real meaning, and we can have real knowledge through what He has communicated to us.

FRANCIS SCHAEFFER

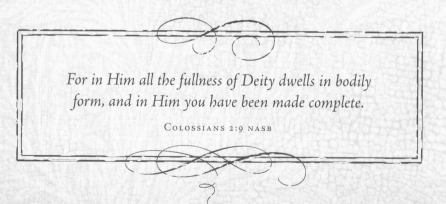

For in Him all the fullness of Deity dwells in bodily form, and in Him you have been made complete.

COLOSSIANS 2:9 NASB

HIS IMPRINT

REST IN HIM

My soul finds rest in God alone; my salvation comes from him. He alone is my rock and my salvation; he is my fortress, I will never be shaken.... My salvation and my honor depend on God; he is my mighty rock, my refuge. Trust in him at all times, O people; pour out your hearts to him, for God is our refuge.... One thing God has spoken, two things have I heard: that you, O God, are strong, and that you, O Lord, are loving.

PSALM 62:1–2, 7–8, 11–12 NIV

Rest in the Lord, and wait patiently for him.

PSALM 37:7 KJV

When God finds a soul that rests in Him and is not easily moved...to this same soul He gives the joy of His presence.

CATHERINE OF GENOA

R E S T   I N   H I M

LIGHT IN THE DARKNESS

There is not enough darkness in all the world to put out the light of one small candle.... In moments of discouragement, defeat, or even despair, there are always certain things to cling to. Little things usually: remembered laughter, the face of a sleeping child, a tree in the wind—in fact, any reminder of something deeply felt or dearly loved. No one is so poor as not to have many of these small candles. When they are lighted, darkness goes away and a touch of wonder remains.

ARTHUR GORDON

One taper lights a thousand,
Yet shines as it has shone;
And the humblest light may kindle
A brighter than its own.

HEZEKIAN BUTTERWORTH

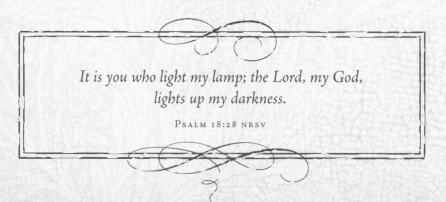

*It is you who light my lamp; the Lord, my God,
lights up my darkness.*

PSALM 18:28 NRSV

LIGHT IN THE DARKNESS

RESTORATION

On the day I called, You answered me; You made me bold with strength in my soul....

For great is the glory of the Lord.... Though I walk in the midst of trouble, You will revive me; You will stretch forth Your hand...and Your right hand will save me. The Lord will accomplish what concerns me; Your lovingkindness, O Lord, is everlasting; do not forsake the works of Your hands.

PSALM 138:3, 5–8 NASB

Weeping may remain for a night, but rejoicing comes in the morning.

PSALM 30:5 NIV

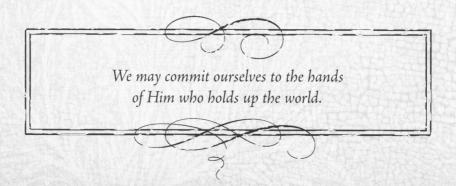

We may commit ourselves to the hands
of Him who holds up the world.

RESTORATION

HIS BEAUTIFUL WORLD

The God who holds the whole world in His hands wraps himself in the splendor of the sun's light and walks among the clouds.

Forbid that I should walk through Thy beautiful world with unseeing eyes:
Forbid that the lure of the market-place should ever entirely steal my heart away from the love of the open acres and the green trees:
Forbid that under the low roof of workshop or office or study I should ever forget Thy great overarching sky.

JOHN BAILLIE

Our Creator would never have made such lovely days, and given us the deep hearts to enjoy them, above and beyond all thought, unless we were meant to be immortal.

NATHANIEL HAWTHORNE

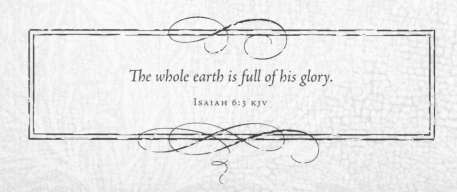

The whole earth is full of his glory.

ISAIAH 6:3 KJV

HIS BEAUTIFUL WORLD

THE WORD OF GOD

For as the rain cometh down, and the snow from heaven, and returneth not thither,
but watereth the earth, and maketh it bring forth and bud, that it may give seed to the
sower, and bread to the eater: So shall my word be that goeth forth out of my mouth:
it shall not return unto me void, but it shall accomplish that which I please, and it shall
prosper in the thing whereto I sent it.

ISAIAH 55:10–11 KJV

Not one word has failed of all His good promise.

1 KINGS 8:56 NASB

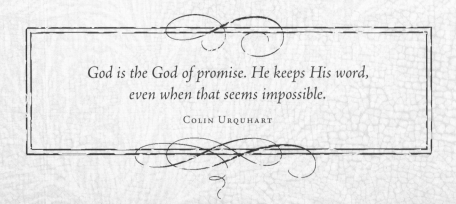

God is the God of promise. He keeps His word,
even when that seems impossible.

COLIN URQUHART

THE WORD OF GOD

_____

_____

_____

_____

_____

_____

_____

_____

_____

_____

_____

_____

_____

_____

_____

_____

_____

_____

_____

_____

_____

_____

_____

Comfort Sweet

There is a place of comfort sweet
Near to the heart of God,
A place where we our Savior meet,
Near to the heart of God....
Hold us who wait before Thee
Near to the heart of God.

Cleland B. McAfee

Not a sigh is breathed, not a pain felt, not a grief pierces the soul, but the throb
vibrates to the Father's heart.

Ellen G. White

God comforts. He lays His right hand on the wounded soul...and He says, as if
that one were the only soul in all the universe: O greatly beloved, fear not: peace
be unto thee.

Amy Carmichael

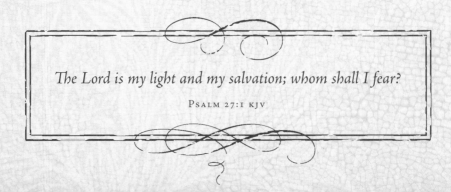

The Lord is my light and my salvation; whom shall I fear?

Psalm 27:1 KJV

COMFORT SWEET

INTERCESSION

If you don't know what you're doing, pray to the Father. He loves to help.

JAMES 1:5 MSG

And the Holy Spirit helps us in our distress. For we don't even know what we
should pray for, nor how we should pray. But the Holy Spirit prays for us with
groanings that cannot be expressed in words. And the Father who knows all hearts
knows what the Spirit is saying, for the Spirit pleads for us believers in harmony
with God's own will. And we know that God causes everything to work together for
the good of those who love God and are called according to his purpose for them.

ROMANS 8:26–28 NLT

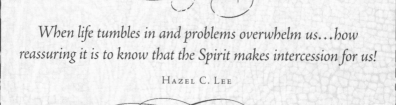

When life tumbles in and problems overwhelm us…how
reassuring it is to know that the Spirit makes intercession for us!

HAZEL C. LEE

INTERCESSION

_____

_____

_____

_____

_____

_____

_____

_____

_____

_____

_____

_____

_____

_____

_____

_____

_____

_____

_____

_____

_____

EVERY NEED

God wants nothing from us except our needs, and these furnish Him with room to display His bounty when He supplies them freely.... Not what I have, but what I do not have, is the first point of contact between my soul and God.

CHARLES H. SPURGEON

Jesus Christ has brought every need, every joy, every gratitude, every hope of ours before God. He accompanies us and brings us into the presence of God.

DIETRICH BONHOEFFER

The "air" which our souls need also envelops all of us at all times and on all sides. God is round about us...on every hand, with many-sided and all-sufficient grace.

OLE HALLESBY

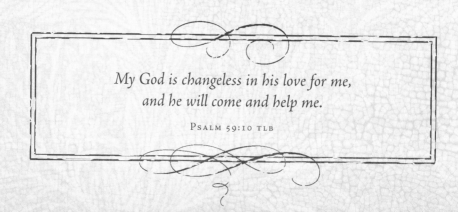

My God is changeless in his love for me, and he will come and help me.

PSALM 59:10 TLB

EVERY NEED

My Help

I will lift up mine eyes unto the hills, from whence cometh my help. My help cometh from the Lord, which made heaven and earth. He will not suffer thy foot to be moved: he that keepeth thee will not slumber. Behold, he that keepeth Israel shall neither slumber nor sleep. The Lord is thy keeper: the Lord is thy shade upon thy right hand. The sun shall not smite thee by day, nor the moon by night. The Lord shall preserve thee from all evil: he shall preserve thy soul. The Lord shall preserve thy going out and thy coming in from this time forth, and even for evermore.

PSALM 121:1–8 KJV

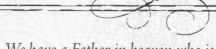

We have a Father in heaven who is almighty, who loves His children as He loves His only-begotten Son, and whose very joy and delight it is to…help them at all times and under all circumstances.

GEORGE MÜELLER

My Help

GOD LISTENS

Open wide the windows of our spirits and fill us full of light; open wide the door of our hearts, that we may receive and entertain Thee with all our powers of adoration.

CHRISTINA ROSSETTI

We come this morning—
Like empty pitchers to a full fountain,
With no merits of our own,
O Lord—open up a window of heaven…
And listen this morning.

JAMES WELDON JOHNSON

God listens in compassion and love, just like we do when our children come to us. He delights in our presence.

RICHARD J. FOSTER

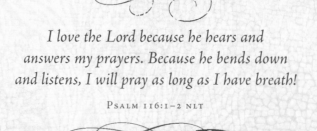

I love the Lord because he hears and answers my prayers. Because he bends down and listens, I will pray as long as I have breath!

PSALM 116:1–2 NLT

GOD LISTENS

GOD IS OUR SHIELD

Trust the Lord! He is your helper; he is your shield.

PSALM 115:9 NLT

Many are saying to me, "There is no help for you in God." But you, O Lord, are a shield around me, my glory, and the one who lifts up my head. I cry aloud to the Lord, and he answers me from his holy hill.

PSALM 3:2–4 NRSV

Let the beloved of the Lord rest secure in him, for he shields him all day long, and the one the Lord loves rests between his shoulders.

DEUTERONOMY 33:12 NIV

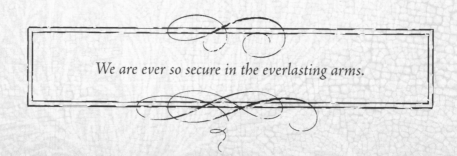

We are ever so secure in the everlasting arms.

GOD IS OUR SHIELD

Always There

We need never shout across the spaces to an absent God. He is nearer than our own soul, closer than our most secret thoughts.

A. W. Tozer

God is always present in the temple of your heart…His home. And when you come in to meet Him there, you find that it is the one place of deep satisfaction where every longing is met.

Always be in a state of expectancy, and see that you leave room for God to come in as He likes.

Oswald Chambers

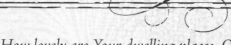

How lovely are Your dwelling places, O Lord of hosts! My soul longed and even yearned for the courts of the Lord; my heart and my flesh sing for joy to the living God…. For a day in Your courts is better than a thousand outside.

Psalm 84:1–2, 10 nasb

ALWAYS THERE

The Goodness of God

I would have despaired unless I had believed that I would see the goodness of the Lord in the land of the living. Wait for the Lord; be strong and let your heart take courage; yes, wait for the Lord.

PSALM 27:13–14 NASB

Be strong and courageous! Do not be afraid…! The Lord your God will go ahead of you. He will neither fail you nor forsake you.

DEUTERONOMY 31:6 NLT

He loveth righteousness and judgment:
the earth is full of the goodness of the Lord.

PSALM 33:5 KJV

God is not merely good, but goodness;
goodness is not merely divine, but God.

C. S. LEWIS

THE GOODNESS OF GOD

_____
_____
_____
_____
_____
_____
_____
_____
_____
_____
_____
_____
_____
_____
_____
_____
_____
_____
_____
_____
_____
_____

PERFECT PEACE

Trials…may come in abundance. But they cannot penetrate into the sanctuary of the soul when it is settled in God, and we may dwell in perfect peace.

HANNAH WHITALL SMITH

What a friend we have in Jesus,

All our sins and griefs to bear;

What a privilege to carry

Everything to God in prayer.

O, what peace we often forfeit,

O, what needless pain we bear,

All because we do not carry

Everything to God in prayer.

GEORGE SCRIVEN

Night by night I will lie down and sleep in the thought of God.

WILLIAM MOUNTFORD

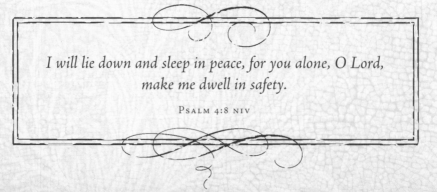

I will lie down and sleep in peace, for you alone, O Lord,
make me dwell in safety.

PSALM 4:8 NIV

PERFECT PEACE

HOPE IN GOD

Why are you in despair, O my soul? And why have you become disturbed within me?

Hope in God, for I shall again praise Him for the help of His presence. O my God, my soul is in despair within me; therefore I remember You.… Deep calls to deep at the sound of Your waterfalls; all Your breakers and Your waves have rolled over me. The Lord will command His lovingkindness in the daytime; and His song will be with me in the night, a prayer to the God of my life.

PSALM 42:5–8 NASB

He will not crush those who are weak or quench the smallest hope.

ISAIAH 42:3 NLT

Hope is faith holding out its hands in the dark.

GEORGE ILES

HOPE IN GOD

Solitude liberates us from entanglements by carving out a space from which we can see ourselves and our situation before the Audience of One. Solitude provides the private place where we can take our bearings and so make God our North Star.

OS GUINNESS

Settle yourself in solitude and you will come upon Him in yourself.

TERESA OF AVILA

We must drink deeply from the very Source the deep calm and peace of interior quietude and refreshment of God, allowing the pure water of divine grace to flow plentifully and unceasingly from the Source itself.

MOTHER TERESA

Whoever drinks of the water that I will give him shall never thirst; but the water that I will give him will become in him a well of water springing up to eternal life.

JOHN 4:13–14 NASB

SETTLED IN SOLITUDE

FREE TO LIVE

God, your God, will cut away the thick calluses on your heart and your children's hearts, freeing you to love God, your God, with your whole heart and soul and live, really live.... And you will make a new start, listening obediently to God, keeping all his commandments that I'm commanding you today. God, your God, will outdo himself in making things go well for you.... Love God, your God. Walk in his ways. Keep his commandments, regulations, and rules so that you will live, really live, live exuberantly, blessed by God.... Love God, your God, listening obediently to him, firmly embracing him. Oh yes, he is life itself.

DEUTERONOMY 30:6–9, 16, 20 MSG

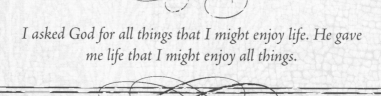

*I asked God for all things that I might enjoy life. He gave
me life that I might enjoy all things.*

FREE TO LIVE

SOUGHT AND FOUND

It is God's will that we believe that we see Him continually, though it seems to us that the sight be only partial; and through this belief He makes us always to gain more grace, for God wishes to be seen, and He wishes to be sought, and He wishes to be expected, and He wishes to be trusted.

JULIAN OF NORWICH

To seek God means first of all to let yourself be found by Him.

God's nature is given me. His love is jealous for my life. All His attributes are woven into the pattern of my spirit. What a God is this! His life implanted in every child. Thank you, Father, for this.

JIM ELLIOT

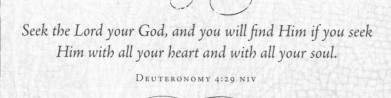

Seek the Lord your God, and you will find Him if you seek Him with all your heart and with all your soul.

DEUTERONOMY 4:29 NIV

SOUGHT AND FOUND

GOD IS OUR REFUGE

Hear my cry, O God; Give heed to my prayer. From the end of the earth I call to You when my heart is faint; lead me to the rock that is higher than I. For You have been a refuge for me, a tower of strength against the enemy. Let me dwell in Your tent forever; let me take refuge in the shelter of Your wings.

PSALM 61:1–4 NASB

Whom have I in heaven but You? And besides You, I desire nothing on earth. My flesh and my heart may fail, but God is the strength of my heart and my portion forever.... As for me, the nearness of God is my good; I have made the Lord God my refuge.

PSALM 73:25–26, 28 NASB

When God has become...our refuge and our fortress, then we can reach out to Him in the midst of a broken world and feel at home while still on the way.

HENRI J. M. NOUWEN

GOD IS OUR REFUGE

THE BEAUTY OF GOD'S PEACE

In comparison with this big world, the human heart is only a small thing. Though the world is so large, it is utterly unable to satisfy this tiny heart. Our ever growing soul and its capacities can be satisfied only in the infinite God. As water is restless until it reaches its level, so the soul has no peace until it rests in God.

SADHU SUNDAR SINGH

Peace is a margin of power around our daily need. Peace is a consciousness of springs too deep for earthly droughts to dry up.

HARRY EMERSON FOSDICK

Drop Thy still dews of quietness
till all our strivings cease;
take from our souls the strain and stress,
and let our ordered lives confess
the beauty of Thy peace.

JOHN GREENLEAF WHITTIER

Be still, and know that I am God.

PSALM 46:10 KJV

THE BEAUTY OF GOD'S PEACE

_____

_____

_____

_____

_____

_____

_____

_____

_____

_____

_____

_____

_____

_____

_____

_____

_____

_____

_____

_____

_____

A RIVER OF DELIGHTS

Your love, O Lord, reaches to the heavens, your faithfulness to the skies. Your righteousness is like the mighty mountains, your justice like the great deep…. How priceless is your unfailing love! Both high and low among men find refuge in the shadow of your wings. They feast on the abundance of your house; you give them drink from your river of delights. For with you is the fountain of life; in your light we see light.

PSALM 36:5–9 NIV

God's love is like a river springing up in the Divine Substance and flowing endlessly through His creation, filling all things with life and goodness and strength.

THOMAS MERTON

A RIVER of DELIGHTS

He Carries Our Sorrows

Your tears are precious to God. They are like stained-glass windows in the darkness, whose true beauty is revealed only when there is a light within.

There is a sacredness in tears. They are not the mark of weakness, but of power. They speak more eloquently than ten thousand tongues. They are the messengers of overwhelming grief, of deep contrition, and of unspeakable love.

WASHINGTON IRVING

When Jesus…confides to us that
He is "acquainted with
Grief," we listen, for that also is an
Acquaintance of our own.

EMILY DICKINSON

A teardrop on earth summons the King of Heaven.

CHARLES R. SWINDOLL

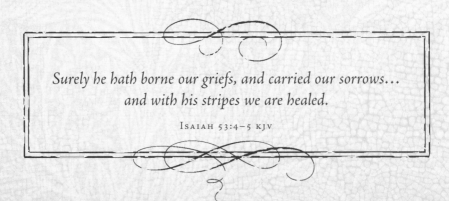

Surely he hath borne our griefs, and carried our sorrows…
and with his stripes we are healed.

ISAIAH 53:4–5 KJV

HE CARRIES OUR SORROWS

_____

_____

_____

_____

_____

_____

_____

_____

_____

_____

_____

_____

_____

_____

_____

_____

_____

_____

_____

_____

I WILL HELP YOU

"So do not fear, for I am with you; do not be dismayed, for I am your God. I will strengthen you and help you; I will uphold you with my righteous right hand. For I am the Lord, your God, who takes hold of your right hand and says to you, Do not fear; I will help you. Do not be afraid…for I myself will help you," declares the Lord, your Redeemer, the Holy One of Israel.

ISAIAH 41:10, 13–14 NIV

For he hath said, I will never leave thee, nor forsake thee. So that we may boldly say, The Lord is my helper, and I will not fear.

HEBREWS 13:5–6 KJV

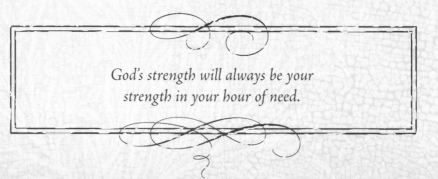

*God's strength will always be your
strength in your hour of need.*

I WILL HELP YOU

NEW EVERY MORNING

Morning has broken like the first morning,

Blackbird has spoken like the first bird....

Praise with elation, praise every morning,

God's re-creation of the new day!

ELEANOR FARJEON

Always new. Always exciting. Always full of promise. The mornings of our lives, each
a personal daily miracle!

GLORIA GAITHER

That is God's call to us—simply to be people who are content

to live close to Him and to renew the kind of life in which the

closeness is felt and experienced.

THOMAS MERTON

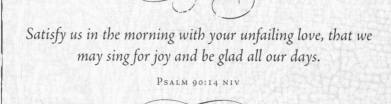

*Satisfy us in the morning with your unfailing love, that we
may sing for joy and be glad all our days.*

PSALM 90:14 NIV

NEW EVERY MORNING

THE LORD'S PRAYER

Our Father which art in heaven, Hallowed be thy name. Thy kingdom come. Thy will be done in earth, as it is in heaven. Give us this day our daily bread. And forgive us our debts, as we forgive our debtors. And lead us not into temptation, but deliver us from evil: For thine is the kingdom, and the power, and the glory, for ever. Amen.

MATTHEW 6:9–13 KJV

They who seek the throne of grace find that throne in every place;
If we live a life of prayer, God is present everywhere.

OLIVER HOLDEN

THE LORD'S PRAYER

SWEET HOUR OF PRAYER

Sweet hour of prayer, sweet hour of prayer,

That calls me from a world of care,

And bids me at my Father's throne,

Make all my wants and wishes known!

In seasons of distress and grief,

My soul has often found relief,

And oft escaped the tempter's snare

By Thy return, sweet hour of prayer.

WILLIAM W. WALFORD

God understands our prayers even when we can't find the words to say them.

If we knew how to listen, we would hear Him speaking to us. For God does speak…. If we knew how to listen to God, if we knew how to look around us, our whole life would become prayer.

MICHAEL QUOIST

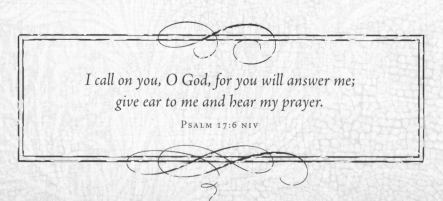

I call on you, O God, for you will answer me;
give ear to me and hear my prayer.

PSALM 17:6 NIV

S W E E T   H O U R   O F   P R A Y E R

FRESH HOPE

God...rekindles burned-out lives with fresh hope, restoring dignity and respect to their lives—a place in the sun! For the very structures of earth are God's; he has laid out his operations on a firm foundation.

1 SAMUEL 2:7–8 MSG

We depend on the Lord alone to save us. Only he can help us, protecting us like a shield. In him our hearts rejoice, for we are trusting in his holy name. Let your unfailing love surround us, Lord, for our hope is in you alone.

PSALM 33:18–22 NLT

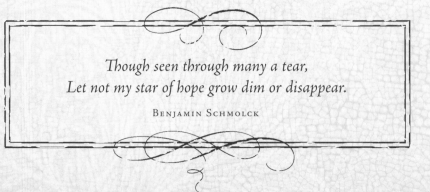

Though seen through many a tear,
Let not my star of hope grow dim or disappear.

BENJAMIN SCHMOLCK

F R E S H   H O P E

FAITHFUL GUIDE

God, who has led you safely on so far, will lead you on to the end. Be altogether at rest in the loving holy confidence which you ought to have in His heavenly Providence.

FRANCIS DE SALES

Guidance is a sovereign act. Not merely does God will to guide us by showing us His way…whatever mistakes we may make, we shall come safely home. Slippings and strayings there will be, no doubt, but the everlasting arms are beneath us; we shall be caught, rescued, restored. This is God's promise; this is how good He is. And our self-distrust, while keeping us humble, must not cloud the joy with which we lean on our faithful covenant God.

J. I. PACKER

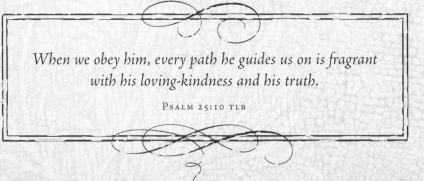

When we obey him, every path he guides us on is fragrant with his loving-kindness and his truth.

PSALM 25:10 TLB

FAITHFUL GUIDE

Seek the Lord

The God who made the world and everything in it is the Lord of heaven and earth.... He himself gives all men life and breath and everything else.... God did this so that men would seek him and perhaps reach out for him and find him, though he is not far from each one of us. "For in him we live, and move, and have our being."

Acts 17:24–28 niv

I love those who love me; and those who diligently seek me will find me.

Proverbs 8:17 nasb

God is not an elusive dream or a phantom to chase, but a divine person to know. He does not avoid us, but seeks us. When we seek Him, the contact is instantaneous.

Neva Coyle

SEEK THE LORD

THAT I MAY KNOW HIM

Lord Jesus Christ…
May I know You more clearly,
Love You more dearly
And follow You more nearly
Day by day. Amen.

RICHARD OF CHINCHESTER

Give us, Lord: a pure heart that we may see Thee, a humble heart that we may hear Thee, a heart of love that we may serve Thee, a heart of faith that we may live with Thee.

DAG HAMMARSKJÖLD

God be in my head, and in my understanding;
God be in my eyes, and in my looking;
God be in my mouth, and in my speaking;
God be in my heart, and in my thinking;
God be at my mine end, and at my departing.

*If you are pleased with me, teach me your ways so I may
know you and continue to find favor with you.*

EXODUS 33:13 NIV

THAT I MAY KNOW HIM

THE LOVE OF GOD

Who shall separate us from the love of Christ? Shall trouble or hardship or persecution or famine or nakedness or danger or sword? No, in all these things we are more than conquerors through him who loved us. For I am convinced that neither death nor life, neither angels nor demons, neither the present nor the future, nor any powers, neither height nor depth, nor anything else in all creation, will be able to separate us from the love of God that is in Christ Jesus our Lord.

ROMANS 8:35, 37–39 NIV

Nothing can separate you from His love, absolutely nothing…. God is enough for time, and God is enough for eternity. God is enough!

HANNAH WHITALL SMITH

THE LOVE OF GOD

GOD'S ANSWERS

I asked for strength that I might achieve;

I was made weak that I might learn humbly to obey.

I asked for health that I might do greater things;

I was given infirmity that I might do better things.

I asked for riches that I might be wise.

I asked for power that I might feel the need of God.

I asked for all things that I might enjoy all things.

I got nothing that I asked for,

But everything that I had hoped for.

Almost despite myself my unspoken prayers were answered;

I am, among all people, most richly blessed.

UNKNOWN CONFEDERATE SOLDIER

We shall come one day to a heaven where we shall gratefully know that God's great refusals were sometimes the true answers to our truest prayer.

P.T. FORSYTH

*For now we see in a mirror dimly , but then face to face;
now I know in part, but then I will know fully just as I also
have been fully known.*

1 CORINTHIANS 13:12 NASB

GOD'S ANSWERS

DELIGHT IN THE LORD

Delight yourself in the Lord and he will give you the desires of your heart. Commit your way to the Lord; trust in him and he will do this: He will make your righteousness shine like the dawn, the justice of your cause like the noonday sun.

PSALM 37:4–6 NIV

Send forth your light and your truth, let them guide me; let them bring me to your holy mountain, to the place where you dwell. Then will I go to the altar of God, to God, my joy and my delight.

PSALM 43:3–4 NIV

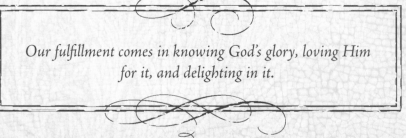

Our fulfillment comes in knowing God's glory, loving Him for it, and delighting in it.

DELIGHT IN THE LORD

TAKE REFUGE

Let my soul take refuge...beneath the shadow of Your wings: let my heart, this sea of restless waves, find peace in You, O God.

AUGUSTINE

My Good Shepherd, who have shown Your very gentle mercy to us,...give grace and strength to me, Your little lamb, that in no tribulation or anguish or pain may I turn away from You.

FRANCIS OF ASSISI

God stands fast as your rock, steadfast as your safeguard, sleepless as your watcher, valiant as your champion.

CHARLES H. SPURGEON

Why would God promise a refuge unless He knew we would need a place to hide once in a while?

NEVA COYLE

The Lord is good, a refuge in times of trouble.
He cares for those who trust in him.

NAHUM 1:7 NIV

TAKE REFUGE

And the Lord God will wipe away tears from off all faces.

ISAIAH 25:8 KJV

We also rejoice in our sufferings, because we know that suffering produces perseverance; perseverance, character; and character, hope. And hope does not disappoint us, because God has poured out his love into our hearts by the Holy Spirit, whom he has given us.

ROMANS 5:3–5 NIV

That I may know him, and the power of his resurrection, and the fellowship of his sufferings.

PHILIPPIANS 3:10 KJV

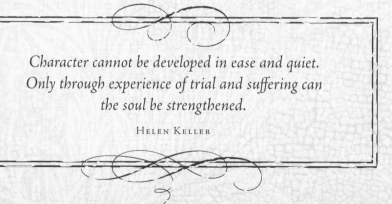

Character cannot be developed in ease and quiet.
Only through experience of trial and suffering can
the soul be strengthened.

HELEN KELLER

STRENGTH IN SUFFERING

TOTALLY AWARE

God is every moment totally aware of each one of us. Totally aware in intense concentration and love…. No one passes through any area of life, happy or tragic, without the attention of God with him.

EUGENIA PRICE

Because God is responsible for our welfare, we are told to cast all our care upon Him, for He cares for us. God says, "I'll take the burden—don't give it a thought—leave it to Me." God is keenly aware that we are dependent upon Him for life's necessities.

BILLY GRAHAM

You are God's created beauty and the focus of His affection and delight.

JANET L. WEAVER SMITH

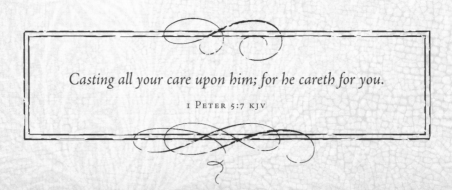

Casting all your care upon him; for he careth for you.

1 PETER 5:7 KJV

TOTALLY AWARE

_____

_____

_____

_____

_____

_____

_____

_____

_____

_____

_____

_____

_____

_____

_____

_____

_____

_____

_____

EVERLASTING LIGHT

The sun will no more be your light by day, nor will the brightness of the moon shine on you, for the Lord will be your everlasting light, and your God will be your glory. Your sun will never set again, and your moon will wane no more; the Lord will be your everlasting light, and your days of sorrow will end.

ISAIAH 60:19–20 NIV

Light arises in the darkness for the upright; He is gracious and compassionate and righteous.

PSALM 112:4 NASB

*Those who have met God are not looking for something—
they have found it; they are not searching for light—upon
them the Light has already shined.*

A.W. TOZER

E V E R L A S T I N G   L I G H T

_____

_____

_____

_____

_____

_____

_____

_____

_____

_____

_____

_____

_____

_____

_____

_____

_____

_____

WAITING QUIETLY

The best reason to pray is that God is really there. In praying, our unbelief gradually starts to melt. God moves smack into the middle of even an ordinary day…. Prayer is a matter of keeping at it…. Thunderclaps and lightning flashes are very unlikely. It is well to start small and quietly.

EMILY GRIFFIN ·

In waiting we begin to get in touch with the rhythms of life—stillness and action, listening and decision. They are the rhythms of God. It is in the everyday and the commonplace that we learn patience, acceptance, and contentment.

RICHARD J. FOSTER

When you get into a tight place and everything goes against you, till it seems as though you could not hang on a minute longer, never give up then, for that is just the place and time that the tide will turn.

HARRIET BEECHER STOWE

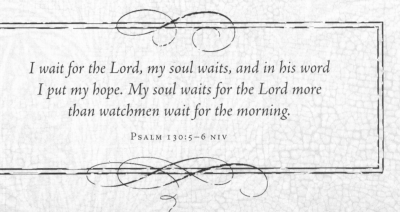

I wait for the Lord, my soul waits, and in his word
I put my hope. My soul waits for the Lord more
than watchmen wait for the morning.

PSALM 130:5–6 NIV

WAITING QUIETLY

GOD'S SOVEREIGNTY

Even though the fig trees have no blossoms, and there are no grapes on the vine;
even though the olive crop fails, and the fields lie empty and barren; even though the
flocks die in the fields, and the cattle barns are empty, yet I will rejoice in the Lord! I
will be joyful in the God of my salvation. The Sovereign Lord is my strength!

HABAKKUK 3:17–19 NLT

Wealth and honor come from you; you are the ruler of all things. In your hands
are strength and power to exalt and give strength to all. Now, our God, we give you
thanks, and praise your glorious name.

1 CHRONICLES 29:12–13 NIV

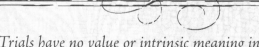

Trials have no value or intrinsic meaning in themselves.
It's the way we respond to those trials
that makes all the difference.

JONI EARECKSON TADA

GOD'S SOVEREIGNTY

THE SEA REMAINS THE SEA

Dear Lord, today I thought of the words of Vincent van Gogh, "It is true that there is an ebb and flow, but the sea remains the sea." You are the sea. Although I may experience many ups and downs in my emotions and often feel great shifts in my inner life, you remain the same…. There are days of sadness and days of joy; there are feelings of guilt and feelings of gratitude; there are moments of failure and moments of success; but all of them are embraced by your unwavering love.

My only real temptation is to doubt your love…to remove myself from the healing radiance of your love. To do these things is to move into the darkness of despair.

O Lord, sea of love and goodness, let me not fear too much the storms and winds of my daily life, and let me know that there is ebb and flow…but that the sea remains the sea. Amen.

HENRI J. M. NOUWEN

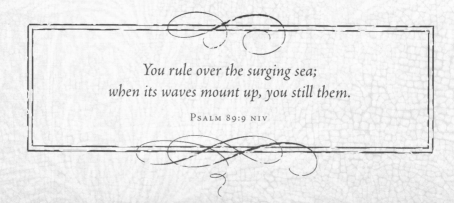

You rule over the surging sea;
when its waves mount up, you still them.

PSALM 89:9 NIV

THE SEA REMAINS THE SEA

_____

_____

_____

_____

_____

_____

_____

_____

_____

_____

_____

_____

_____

_____

_____

_____

_____

_____

_____

WONDERFUL JOY AHEAD

All honor to the God and Father of our Lord Jesus Christ, for it is by his boundless mercy that God has given us the privilege of being born again. Now we live with a wonderful expectation because Jesus Christ rose again from the dead…. So be truly glad! There is wonderful joy ahead, even though it is necessary for you to endure many trials for a while…. These trials are only to test your faith, to show that it is strong and pure. It is being tested as fire tests and purifies gold—and your faith is far more precious to God than mere gold. So if your faith remains strong after being tried by fiery trials, it will bring you much praise and glory and honor on the day when Jesus Christ is revealed.

1 PETER 1:3, 6–7 NLT

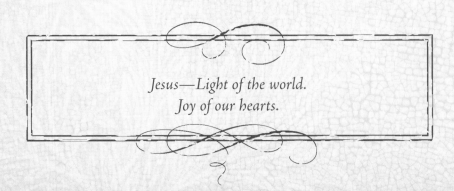

Jesus—Light of the world.
Joy of our hearts.

WONDERFUL JOY AHEAD

_____

_____

_____

_____

_____

_____

_____

_____

_____

_____

_____

_____

_____

_____

_____

_____

_____

_____

_____

_____

OVERFLOWING PRAISE

All enjoyment spontaneously overflows into praise.... The world rings with praise...
walkers praising the countryside, players praising their favorite game....
I think we delight to praise what we enjoy because the praise not merely expresses
but completes the enjoyment; it is the appointed consummation.

C. S. LEWIS

God's pursuit of praise from us and our pursuit of pleasure in Him are one and the
same pursuit. God's quest to be glorified and our quest to be satisfied reach their
goal in this one experience: our delight in God which overflows in praise.

JOHN PIPER

Earth, with her thousand voices, praises God.

SAMUEL TAYLOR COLERIDGE

O sing unto the Lord a new song:
sing unto the Lord, all the earth.

PSALM 96:1 KJV

OVERFLOWING PRAISE

No More Tears

And I heard a loud voice from the throne saying, "Now the dwelling of God is with men, and he will live with them. They will be his people, and God himself will be with them and be their God. He will wipe every tear from their eyes. There will be no more death or mourning or crying or pain, for the old order of things has passed away." He who was seated on the throne said, "I am making everything new.... I am the Alpha and the Omega, the Beginning and the End."

REVELATION 21:3–6 NIV

The implications of the name Immanuel are comforting....
He desires to weep with us and to wipe away our tears.

MICHAEL CARD

N O   M O R E   T E A R S

The God of All Comfort

We may ask, "Why does God bring thunderclouds and disasters when we want green pastures and still waters?" Bit by bit, we find behind the clouds, the Father's feet; behind the lightning, an abiding day that has no night; behind the thunder, a still small voice that comforts with a comfort that is unspeakable.

Oswald Chambers

Regardless of the need, God comforts. He is the God of all comfort! That's His specialty.

Charles R. Swindoll

God walks with us.... He scoops us up in His arms or simply sits with us in silent strength until we cannot avoid the awesome recognition that yes, even now, He is here.

Gloria Gaither

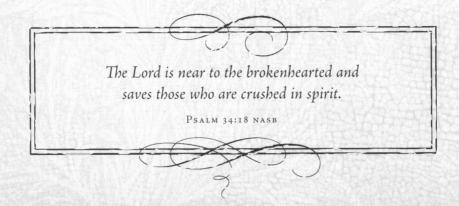

*The Lord is near to the brokenhearted and
saves those who are crushed in spirit.*

Psalm 34:18 nasb

THE GOD OF ALL COMFORT

_____

_____

_____

_____

_____

_____

_____

_____

_____

_____

_____

_____

_____

_____

_____

_____

_____

_____

_____

_____

_____

_____

PRAISE AND WORSHIP

Praise ye the Lord. Praise God in his sanctuary: praise him in the firmament of his power. Praise him for his mighty acts: praise him according to his excellent greatness. Praise him with the sound of the trumpet: praise him with the psaltery and harp. Praise him with the timbrel and dance: praise him with stringed instruments and organs. Praise him upon the loud cymbals: praise him upon the high sounding cymbals. Let every thing that hath breath praise the Lord. Praise ye the Lord.

PSALM 150:1–6 KJV

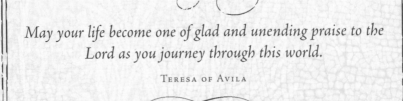

May your life become one of glad and unending praise to the Lord as you journey through this world.

TERESA OF AVILA

PRAISE AND WORSHIP

MAKE ME AN INSTRUMENT

Lord, make me an instrument of Your peace.

Where there is hatred, let me bring love….

Where there is doubt, faith.

Where there is despair, hope.

Where there is sadness, joy.

Where there is darkness, Your light….

O Divine Master, grant that I may not so much

Seek to be consoled as to console;

To be understood as to understand;

To be loved as to love;

For it is in giving that we receive;

It is in pardoning that we are pardoned; and

It is in dying that we are born to eternal life.

FRANCIS OF ASSISI

Our grief always brings a gift. It's the gift of greater sensitivity and compassion for others. We learn to rise above our own grief by reaching out and lessening the grief of others.

ROBERT SCHULLER

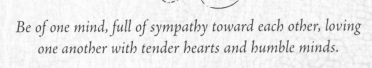

Be of one mind, full of sympathy toward each other, loving
one another with tender hearts and humble minds.

1 PETER 3:8 NLT

MAKE ME AN INSTRUMENT

THE PRESENCE OF GOD

I look behind me and you're there, then up ahead and you're there, too—your reassuring presence, coming and going. This is too much, too wonderful—I can't take it all in!

PSALM 139:5–6 MSG

Where can I go from your Spirit? Where can I flee from your presence? If I go up to the heavens, you are there; if I make my bed in the depths, you are there. If I rise on the wings of the dawn, if I settle on the far side of the sea, even there your hand will guide me, your right hand will hold me fast.

PSALM 139:7–10 NIV

I am with you and will watch over you wherever you go.

GENESIS 28:15 NIV

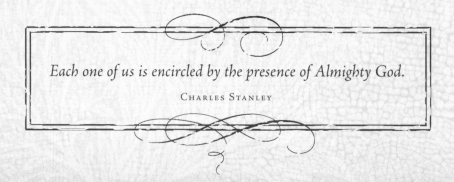

Each one of us is encircled by the presence of Almighty God.

CHARLES STANLEY

THE PRESENCE OF GOD

LOVE ONE ANOTHER

You who have received so much love share it with others. Love others the way that God has loved you, with tenderness.

MOTHER TERESA

Let Jesus be in your heart,

Eternity in your spirit,

The world under your feet,

The will of God in your actions.

And let the love of God shine forth from you.

CATHERINE OF GENOA

Every single act of love bears the imprint of God.

Dear friends, since God so loved us, we also ought to love one another.... If we love one another, God lives in us and his love is made complete in us.

1 JOHN 4:11–12 NIV

LOVE ONE ANOTHER

_____

_____

_____

_____

_____

_____

_____

_____

_____

_____

_____

_____

_____

_____

_____

_____

_____

_____

_____

_____

_____

Whatsoever things are true, whatsoever things are honest, whatsoever things are just, whatsoever things are pure, whatsoever things are lovely, whatsoever things are of good report; if there be any virtue, and if there be any praise, think on these things.

PHILIPPIANS 4:8 KJV

The Lord is in his holy Temple; the Lord still rules from heaven. He watches everything closely, examining everyone on earth…. For the Lord is righteous, and he loves justice. Those who do what is right will see his face.

PSALM 11:4, 7 NLT

The fountain of beauty is the heart, and every generous thought illustrates the walls of your chamber.

FRANCIS QUARLES

The happiness of your life depends upon the character of your thoughts.

T H I N K O N T H E S E T H I N G S

SOURCE OF WONDER

I would maintain that thanks are the highest form of thought, and that gratitude is happiness doubled by wonder.

G. K. CHESTERTON

Dear Lord, grant me the grace of wonder. Surprise me, amaze me, awe me in every crevice of your universe…. Each day enrapture me with your marvelous things without number. I do not ask to see the reason for it all; I ask only to share the wonder of it all.

JOSHUA ABRAHAM HESCHEL

May our lives be illumined
by the steady radiance
renewed daily,
of a wonder,
the source of which
is beyond reason.

DAG HAMMARSKJÖLD

I will give thanks to the Lord with all my heart; I will tell of all Your wonders. I will be glad and exult in You; I will sing praise to Your name, O Most High.

PSALM 9:1–2 NASB

SOURCE OF WONDER

GOD'S NEARNESS

I have sought Thy nearness;
With all my heart have I called Thee,
And going out to meet Thee
I found Thee coming toward me.

YEHUDA HALEVI

O Lord, by all Thy dealings with us, whether of light or darkness, of joy or pain, let us be brought to Thee.

PHILLIPS BROOKS

It is God to whom and with whom we travel, and while He is the End of our journey, He is also at every stopping place.

ELISABETH ELLIOT

Draw near to God and He will draw near to you.

JAMES 4:8 NASB

GOD'S NEARNESS

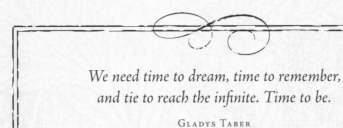

We need time to dream, time to remember,
and tie to reach the infinite. Time to be.

GLADYS TABER